THE INTER
LAWS OF
CONTRACT BRIDGE
1993

THE INTERNATIONAL LAWS OF CONTRACT BRIDGE 1993

as agreed upon and promulgated by
The Portland Club
The European Bridge League
American Contract Bridge League
and approved by
The World Bridge Federation

Published for the Portland Club
by
VICTOR GOLLANCZ LTD
in association with
PETER CRAWLEY

This edition first published in Great Britain 1993
in association with Peter Crawley
by Victor Gollancz Ltd
14 Henrietta Street, London WC2E 8QJ

A catalogue record for this book
is available from the British Library

ISBN 0 575 05252 X

Typeset at Rowland Phototypesetting Ltd
Bury St Edmunds, Suffolk
Printed at St Edmundsbury Press Ltd
Bury St Edmunds, Suffolk

PREFACE TO THE ENGLISH EDITION

The new International Laws of Contract Bridge replace the 1981 Laws of Contract Bridge. The new Laws are effective as from 1st January 1993, but any group may bring them into effect earlier if they so decide.

The Copyright in the British Commonwealth (other than in the Western Hemisphere), the Continent of Africa, in India, Spain, Portugal, and all English-speaking countries in the Eastern Hemisphere, is vested in the Portland Club.

The Copyright in all non-English-speaking countries in Europe (other than Spain and Portugal) is vested in The European Bridge League.

The Copyright in the Western Hemisphere and in the Republic of the Philippines is vested in the American Contract Bridge League.

Extracts from these Laws either verbatim or paraphrased cannot be permitted without the sanction of the Authority holding the Copyright.

Information in respect of these Laws (other than the American Edition) can be obtained from The Portland Club.

The Laws of Contract Bridge as described in this book apply only to Rubber Bridge.

THE PORTLAND CLUB,
HALF MOON STREET,
LONDON SW1.

CARD COMMITTEE OF THE PORTLAND CLUB

J. S. Wheeler, *Chairman*
D. T. H. Davenport
C. G. R. Leach
D. Marchessini

R. S. Brock   *Northern Ireland Bridge Union*
J. G. Faulkner   *English Bridge Union*
P. Jourdain   *Welsh Bridge Union*
J. M. MacLaren   *Scottish Bridge Union*

CONTENTS

THE SCOPE OF THE LAWS

The Laws are designed to define correct procedure and to provide an adequate remedy whenever a player accidentally, carelessly or inadvertently disturbs the proper course of the game, or gains an unintentional but nevertheless unfair advantage. An offending player should be ready to pay a prescribed penalty graciously.

These Laws do not deal with dishonourable practices; ostracism is the ultimate remedy.

THE PROPRIETIES

The object of the Proprieties is to familiarise players with the customs and etiquette of the game, generally accepted over many years; and to enlighten those who might otherwise fail to appreciate when or how they are improperly conveying information to their partners, or are acting on the basis of improper information.

APPENDICES

Most players will find the Laws and the Proprieties sufficient to their needs. Some, however, may wish to adopt procedures to reduce the risk that, unintentionally, extraneous information is given to partners, or proper information withheld from opponents. Possible procedures, very similar to those successfully used in competitive bridge, are set out in appendices 1, 2 and 3. Note that these appendices are not part of the Laws or the Proprieties of Rubber Bridge.

PART I

DEFINITIONS

AUCTION – 1. The process of determining the contract by means of successive calls. 2. The aggregate of calls made.

BID – An undertaking to win at least a specified number of odd tricks in a specified denomination.

CALL – Any bid, double, redouble or pass.

CONTRACT – The undertaking by declarer's side to win, at the denomination named, the number of odd tricks specified in the final bid, whether undoubled, doubled or redoubled.

DEAL – 1. The distribution of the pack to form the hands of the four players. 2. The cards so distributed as a unit, including the auction and play thereof.

DECLARER – The player who, for the side that makes the final bid, first bid the denomination named in that bid. He becomes declarer when a legal opening lead is made, and the dummy is faced.

DEFENDER – An opponent of declarer.

DENOMINATION – The suit or notrump specified in a bid.

DOUBLE – A call over an opponent's bid increasing the scoring value of fulfilled or defeated contracts (*see* Law 19).

DUMMY – 1. Declarer's partner. 2. Declarer's partner's cards, once they are spread on the table after the opening lead.

FOLLOW SUIT – Play a card of the suit that has been led.

GAME – A unit in scoring denoting 100 or more trick points scored on one deal, or accumulated over two or more deals (*see* Laws 72 and 73).

GROUP – A number of players who have agreed to follow the same procedures.

HAND – The cards originally dealt to a player, or the remaining portion thereof.

HONOUR – Any Ace, King, Queen, Jack or ten.

IRREGULARITY – A deviation from the correct procedures set forth in these Laws.

LHO – Left-hand opponent.

LEAD – The first card played to a trick.

ODD TRICK – Each trick to be won by declarer's side in excess of six.

OPENING LEAD – The card led to the first trick.

OPPONENT – A member of the partnership to which one is opposed.

OVERTRICK – Each trick won by declarer's side in excess of the contract.

PACK – The 52 playing cards with which the game of Contract Bridge is played.

PARTNER – The player with whom one plays as a side against the other two players.

PART SCORE – 90 or fewer trick points.

PASS – A call specifying that a player does not, at that turn, elect to bid, double or redouble.

PENALTY – An obligation or restriction imposed upon a side for violation of these Laws.

PENALTY CARD – A card prematurely exposed by a defender. It may be a major or minor penalty card (see Law 50).

PLAY – 1. The contribution of a card from one's hand to a trick, including the first card, which is the lead. 2. The aggregate of plays made. 3. The period during which the cards are played, starting immediately after the final pass.

RHO – Right-hand opponent.

REDEAL – A second or subsequent deal to replace a faulty deal.

REDOUBLE – A call over an opponent's double increasing the

scoring value of fulfilled or defeated contracts (*see* Law 19).

REVOKE – The play of a card of another suit by a player who is able to follow suit or to comply with a lead penalty.

ROTATION – The clockwise order in which the right to deal, to call or to play progresses.

RUBBER – The scoring period that ends when one side has scored two games.

SIDE – Two players who constitute a partnership against the other two players.

SLAM – A contract to win twelve tricks (called Small Slam) or thirteen tricks (called Grand Slam).

SUIT – One of four groups of cards in the pack, each group comprising thirteen cards and having a characteristic symbol: Spades (♠), Hearts (♡), Diamonds (♢), Clubs (♣).

TRICK – The unit by which the outcome of the contract is determined, regularly consisting of four cards, one contributed by each player in rotation, beginning with the lead.

TRUMP – Each card of the suit, if any, named in the contract.

UNDERTRICK – Each trick by which declarer's side falls short of fulfilling the contract.

VULNERABLE – The status of a side that has won a game and is therefore exposed to greater undertrick penalties and entitled to greater premiums.

PART II

PRELIMINARIES

Law
1. The Players – the Pack
Contract Bridge is played by four players with a pack of 52 cards of identical back design and colour, consisting of thirteen cards in each of four suits. Two packs should be used, of which only one is in play at any time; and each pack should be clearly distinguishable from the other in back design or colour.

2. Rank of Cards
The suits rank downwards in order – Spades (♠), Hearts (♡), Diamonds (♢), Clubs (♣). The cards of each suit rank in descending order: Ace, King, Queen, Jack, 10, 9, 8, 7, 6, 5, 4, 3, 2.

3. The Draw
Before every rubber, each player draws a card from a pack shuffled and spread face down on the table. A card should not be exposed until all the players have drawn.

Unless it is otherwise agreed, the two players who draw the highest cards play as partners against the other two players. When cards of the same rank are drawn, the rank of suit determines which is higher.

The player with the highest card deals first and has the right to choose his seat and the pack with which he will deal. He may consult his partner, but having announced his decision must abide by it. His partner sits opposite him. The opponents then occupy the two remaining seats as they wish, and having made their selection must abide by it.

A player must draw again if he draws more than one card, or one of the four cards at either end of the pack, or a card adjoining one drawn by another player, or a card from the other pack.

PART III

THE DEAL

Law
4. The Shuffle

Before the first deal of a rubber, the player to the dealer's left should shuffle the pack thoroughly,* without exposing the face of any card, in full view of the players and to their satisfaction. Thereafter, as each player deals, the dealer's partner shuffles the other pack for the next deal, and places the pack face down on his right.

A pack properly prepared should not be disturbed until the dealer picks it up for his deal, at which time he is entitled to the final shuffle.

No player other than the dealer and the player designated to prepare the pack may shuffle.

5. The Cut

The pack must be cut immediately before it is dealt. The dealer presents the pack to his RHO, who lifts off a portion and places it on the table toward the dealer. Each portion must contain at least four cards. The dealer completes the cut by placing what was originally the bottom portion upon the other portion.

No player other than the dealer's RHO may cut the pack.

6. New Cut – New Shuffle

There must be a new cut if any player demands one before

---

* It is recommended that the pack be shuffled at least five times.

the first card is dealt. In this case, the dealer's RHO cuts again.

There must be a new shuffle followed by a cut:

(a) If any player demands one before the dealer has picked up the pack for his deal. In this case, the player designated to prepare the pack shuffles again.

(b) If any player demands one after the dealer has picked up the pack but before the first card is dealt. In this case only the dealer shuffles.

(c) If a card is turned face up in shuffling. In this case the player who was shuffling shuffles again.

(d) If a card is turned face up in cutting. In this case only the dealer shuffles.

(e) If there is a redeal (*see* Law 10).

7. Change of Pack

The two packs are used alternately, unless there is a redeal.

A pack containing a card so damaged or marked that it may be identified from its back must be replaced* if attention is drawn to the imperfection before the last card of the current deal has been dealt.

A pack originally belonging to a side must be restored on demand of any player before the last card of the current deal has been dealt.*

8. The Deal

The dealer distributes the cards face down, one at a time in rotation into four separate hands of thirteen cards each, the first card to the player on his left and the last card to himself. If he deals two cards simultaneously or consecutively to the same player, or fails to deal a card to a player, he may rectify the error, provided he does so immediately and to the satisfaction of the other players.

* *See* Law 8.

The dealer must not allow the face of any card to be seen while he is dealing.

Players should not look at the face of any card until the deal is completed. A player who violates this provision forfeits those rights to a change of pack (Law 7) or redeal (Law 10).

9. Rotation of the Turn to Deal

The turn to deal passes in rotation unless there is a redeal. If a player deals out of turn, and attention is not drawn to the error before the last card has been dealt, the deal stands as though it had been in turn, the player who dealt the cards is the dealer (he makes the first call), and the player who missed his turn to deal has no redress; and the rotation continues as though the deal had been in turn, unless a redeal is required under Law 10.

10. Redeal

A redeal cancels the faulty deal; the same dealer deals again, unless he was dealing out of turn; the same pack is used, unless it has been replaced as provided in Law 7; and the cards are shuffled and cut anew as provided in Laws 4 and 5.

There must be a redeal:

(a) If, before the last card has been dealt, it is discovered that

>   (i) a card has been turned face up in dealing or is face up in the pack or elsewhere;
>   (ii) the cards have not been dealt correctly;*
>   (iii) a player is dealing out of turn or is dealing with a pack that was not shuffled or not cut, provided any player* demands a redeal.

(b) If, before the first call has been made, it is discovered

* *See* Law 8.

that a player has picked up another player's hand and has seen a card in it.

(c) If, before play has been completed, it is discovered that

(i) the pack did not conform in every respect to the requirements of Law 1, including any case in which a missing card cannot be found after due search;

(ii) one player has picked up too many cards, another too few;

(iii) two or more players on opposing sides have allowed any cards from their hands to be mixed together, following a claim that a redeal is in order.

11. Missing Card

When a player has too few cards and a redeal is not required by Law 10(c), the deal stands as correct, *and*:

(a) If he has played more than one card to a previous trick, Law 67 applies;

(b) If a missing card is found elsewhere, not in a previous trick, that card is deemed to have belonged continuously to the deficient hand and must be restored to that hand; it may become a penalty card, as provided in Law 23 or 49, and failure to have played it may constitute a revoke.

12. Surplus Card

When a player has too many cards and a redeal is not required by Law 10(c) the deal stands as correct, *and*

(a) If the offender has omitted to play to a trick, Law 67 applies.

(b) If the offender has picked up a surplus card from a previous trick, or from dummy's hand, or from the other pack, or elsewhere, such surplus card shall be restored to its proper place; *and*

(i) if the surplus card is in the offender's hand when it is discovered, there is no penalty.

(ii) if the surplus card has been led or played, or had been played to a previous trick, the offender must substitute for it a card from his hand that he can legally play to the trick and, if possible, a card of the same suit as the surplus card. The offending side may not thereby win a trick it had lost, but it may lose a trick it had won. When attention is drawn to the offence before the lead to the next trick, either member of the non-offending side may, without penalty, withdraw a play made subsequent to the offence, and substitute any legal play.

PART IV

GENERAL LAWS GOVERNING IRREGULARITIES

Law
13. Procedure Following an Irregularity
When an irregularity has occurred, any player – except dummy as restricted by Law 43 – may draw attention to it and give or obtain information as to the law applicable to it. The fact that a player draws attention to an irregularity committed by his side does not affect the rights of the opponents.

After attention has been drawn to an irregularity, no player should call or play until all questions in regard to the assessment of a penalty have been determined. Premature correction of an irregularity on the part of the offender may subject him to further penalty (*see* Law 26).

14. Assessment of a Penalty
A penalty may not be imposed until the nature of the irregularity to be penalised has been determined and the applicable penalty has been clearly stated; but a penalty once paid, or any decision agreed and acted upon by the players, stands and should not, except by agreement of all four players, be corrected even though at some later time it may be judged incorrect.

15. Waiver or Forfeiture of Penalty
The right to penalise an offence is forfeited if
   (a) both members of the non-offending side waive the penalty;

(b) a member of the non-offending side calls (Law 34) or plays (Law 60) after an irregularity committed by his RHO.

16. Unauthorised Information

A player may be subject to penalty if he conveys information to his partner other than by a legal call or play.

Information conveyed by an illegal call, play or exposure of a card is subject to the applicable law in Part V or VI.

If a player conveys information to his partner by means of a remark or question or by an unmistakable hesitation or unwonted speed , special emphasis, tone, gesture, movement, mannerism or any other action that suggests a call, lead or plan of play; and if attention is drawn to the offence immediately, when the offending side has profited through the doubtful call or play so suggested, it should, in conformance with Proprieties 1, redress any damage done to the non-offending side.

PART V

THE AUCTION
CORRECT PROCEDURE

Law
17. Duration of the Auction
The auction begins when the last card of a correct deal has been placed on the table. The dealer makes the first call, and thereafter each player calls in rotation. When three passes in rotation have followed any call the auction is closed, unless Law 34 applies.

18. Bids
Each bid* must name a number of odd tricks, from one to seven, and a denomination. A bid supersedes the previous bid if it names either a greater number of odd tricks or the same number of odd tricks in a higher denomination. A bid that fulfils these requirements is sufficient; one that does not is insufficient. The denominations rank in descending order: notrump, spades, hearts, diamonds, clubs.

19. Doubles and Redoubles
A player may double only the last preceding bid, and then only if it was made by an opponent and no calls other than pass have intervened.

A player may redouble only the last preceding double, and then only if it was made by an opponent and no calls other than pass have intervened.

A player should not, in doubling or redoubling, state the

* Pass, double and redouble are calls, not bids.

number of tricks or the denomination; but, if he states either or both incorrectly, he is deemed to have doubled or re-doubled the bid as it was made. The only correct form is the single word 'Double' or 'Redouble'.

All doubles and redoubles are superseded by a subsequent legal bid. If there is no subsequent bid, scoring values are increased as provided in Law 81.

20. Review and Explanation

A player who does not hear a call distinctly may forthwith require that it be repeated.

At his own turn to call during the auction, a player (unless required by law to pass) may require a restatement of the auction in its entirety.

After the final pass, declarer before making any play, or either defender at his first turn to play, may require a restatement of the auction in its entirety.

A request to have calls restated should be responded to only by an opponent (dummy, or a player required by law to pass, may so respond). All players, including dummy, should promptly correct errors in restatement.

A player may require an explanation of the partnership understanding relating to any call made by an opponent, but only at the player's own turn to call or play. A request for an explanation of a call should be responded to by the partner of the player making the call (see Proprieties 4).

21. Call Based on Misinformation

A player has no recourse if he has made a call on the basis of his own misunderstanding.

Until the auction is closed, a player may, without penalty, change any call he may have made as a result of misinformation given him by an opponent, provided his partner has not subsequently called. If he elects to correct his call, his LHO may then, in turn and without penalty, change any subsequent call he may have made.

22. *Procedure After the Auction is Closed*

After the auction is closed:

(a) If no player has bid, the hands are abandoned and the turn to deal passes in rotation.

(b) If any player has bid, the final bid becomes the contract and play begins.

IRREGULARITIES

23. *Card Exposed or Led During the Auction*

Whenever, during the auction, a player faces a card on the table or holds a card so that it is possible for his partner to see its face, every such card must be left face up on the table until the auction closes; and (*penalty*) if the offender subsequently becomes a defender, declarer may treat every such card as a penalty card (Law 50).

In addition:

(a) If it is a single card below the rank of an honour and not prematurely led, there is no further penalty.

(b) If it is a single card of honour rank, or any card prematurely led, or if more than one card is so exposed, (*penalty*) the offender's partner must pass when next it is his turn to call.

(c) When the penalty under this or any other Law compels the offender's partner to pass, and offender could have known at the time of his infraction that the enforced pass would be likely to damage the non-offending side, the offenders should redress the damage in accordance with Proprieties 1.

24. *Immediate Correction of a Call*

A player may substitute his intended call for an inadvertent call, but only if he does so, or attempts to do so, without pause for thought. If legal, his last call stands without penalty; if illegal, it is subject to the applicable law.

25. Change of Call

When a call is substituted for a call made previously at the same turn, and it is too late for correction as provided in Law 24, then:

(a) If the first call was illegal, the substitute call is cancelled and the offender is subject to the applicable law.

(b) If the first call was a legal one, the offender must either

(i) allow his first call to stand and (*penalty*) his partner must pass when next it is his turn to call; *or*

(ii) make any other legal call and (*penalty*) his partner must pass whenever it is his turn to call.

The offender's partner will also be subject to a lead penalty as provided in Law 26 if he becomes a defender. Law 23(c) may apply to (b)(i) and (b)(ii).

26. Change of Call – Lead Penalties

When a player makes a call and subsequently changes it to another legal call (except as permitted under Law 24), then if he becomes a defender:

(a) If the changed call was in a suit, and the substituted call did not repeat that suit, declarer may* either require the offender's partner to lead, or prohibit him from leading, such suit, when first the offender's partner has the lead (including the opening lead). A prohibition continues for as long as offender's partner retains the lead. When the irregular call artificially relates to a denomination other than the one actually named, 'such suit' is the suit or suits to which the call relates.

(b) If the changed call was

* Declarer makes the decision at the time that offender's partner first has the lead.

(i) in notrump, and his final call at that turn was not; *or*

(ii) pass, double or redouble, other than an out-of-rotation call repeated in turn in accordance with Law 30(a) or 32(b)(i),

declarer may prohibit offender's partner from leading any one specified suit when the first offender's partner has the lead (including the opening lead). This prohibition continues for as long as offender's partner retains the lead.

27. Insufficient Bid

Any insufficient bid may be accepted (treated as legal) at the option of the offender's LHO, and is accepted if that opponent calls.

An insufficient bid made in rotation must be corrected by the substitution of either a sufficient bid (not a double or redouble) or a pass,* unless the irregular bid is accepted.

If the call substituted is

(a) the lowest sufficient bid in the same denomination, the auction proceeds as though the irregularity had not occurred.[†]

(b) any other sufficient bid, or pass, (*penalty*) the offender's partner must pass whenever it is his turn to call (Law 23(c) may apply) and the lead penalties of Law 26 will apply if he becomes a defender.

If the offender attempts to substitute a double or redouble, it is cancelled; he must pass at that turn and the offence is subject to the penalty provided in subsection (b) above.

If a player makes an insufficient bid out of rotation, Law 31 applies.

* The offender is entitled to select his final call at that turn after the applicable penalties have been stated, and any call he has previously attempted to substitute is cancelled, but the lead penalties of Law 26 will apply if he becomes a defender.

[†] Offender's partner must not base any subsequent calls or plays on information gained from such a withdrawn bid.

CALL OUT OF ROTATION

28. Calls Considered to be In Rotation
A call is considered to be in rotation

(a) when it is made without waiting for the RHO to pass, if that opponent is required by law to pass.

(b) when it is made by the player whose turn it was to call, before a penalty has been imposed for a call out of rotation by an opponent; it waives any penalty for the call out of rotation and the auction proceeds as though that opponent had not called at that turn.

29. Procedure After a Call Out of Rotation
After a call out of rotation, offender's LHO* may either:

(a) make any legal call; if he chooses to do so, the call out of rotation stands as if it were legal (but if it is an inadmissible call, *see* Law 35), and the auction proceeds without penalty; *or*

(b) require that the call out of rotation be cancelled. The auction reverts to the player whose turn it was to call. The offender may make any legal call in proper turn subject to Laws 30, 31, and 32.

30. Pass Out of Rotation
When a player has passed out of rotation:

(a) before any player has bid, or when it was the turn of his RHO† to call, (*penalty*) the offender must pass when next it is his turn to call.

(b) after any player has bid and when it was the turn of the offender's partner to call (*penalty*) the offender must pass whenever it is his turn to call; the offender's partner

---

* He alone exercises the option, although any player may draw attention to the irregularity.

† After any player has bid, a call at the turn of offender's LHO is a change of call; Law 25 applies and not this section.

may make a sufficient bid or may pass, but may not double or redouble at that turn.

31. Bid Out of Rotation

When a player has bid out of rotation:

(a) at the turn of offender's partner to call, or before any player has called when offender's LHO was the dealer, (*penalty*) the offender's partner must pass whenever it is his turn to call (Law 23(c) may apply), and the lead penalties of Law 26 will apply if he becomes a defender

(b) at the turn of the offender's RHO* to call

    (i) if RHO passes, the bid out of rotation must be repeated, and there is no penalty (if the bid out of rotation was insufficient, it must be corrected as provided in Law 27);

    (ii) if RHO makes a legal[†] bid, double or redouble, the offender may in turn make any legal call. If such call repeats the denomination of the bid out of rotation, (*penalty*) the offender's partner must pass when next it is his turn to call (Law 23(c) may apply). If the substituted call does not repeat the denomination, (*penalty*) the offender's partner must pass whenever it is his turn to call (Law 23(c) may apply), and the lead penalties of Law 26 will apply if he becomes a defender.

32. Double or Redouble Out of Rotation

When a player has doubled or redoubled out of rotation:

(a) If it was the offender's partner's turn to call, (*penalty*) the offender's partner must pass whenever it is his turn to

---

  * After any player has called, a call at offender's LHO's turn is a change of call; Law 25 applies and not this section.

  † An illegal call by that opponent may be penalized in the usual way, after which this subsection, (b)(ii), applies.

call (Law 23(c) may apply); the offender may not thereafter, in turn, double or redouble the same bid he doubled out of turn; and the lead penalties of Law 26(b) will apply if he becomes a defender.

    (b) If it was the turn of offender's RHO* to call:

        (i) If offender's RHO passes, the double or redouble out of rotation must be repeated and there is no penalty.

        (ii) If offender's RHO bids, the offender may in turn make any legal call, and (*penalty*) the offender's partner must pass when next it is his turn to call (Law 23(c) may apply), and the lead penalties of Law 26(b) will apply if he becomes a defender.

33. *Simultaneous Calls*

A call made simultaneously with one made by the player whose turn it was to call is deemed to be a subsequent call.

34. *Retention of the Right to Call*

When a call has been followed by three passes, the auction does not end when one of those passes was out of rotation, thereby depriving a player of his right to call at that turn. The auction reverts to the player who missed his turn. All subsequent passes are cancelled and the auction proceeds as though there had been no irregularity.

INADMISSIBLE CALLS

35. *Inadmissible Call Condoned*

When after an inadmissible call specified below, offender's

---

  * After any player has called, a call at offender's LHO's turn is a change of call; Law 25 applies and not this section.

LHO makes a call before a penalty has been assessed, there is no penalty for the offence (the lead penalties of Law 26 do not apply). If the inadmissible call was:

(a) a double or redouble not permitted by Law 19, that call and all subsequent calls are cancelled; the auction reverts to the player whose turn it is to call and proceeds as though there had been no irregularity;

(b) a bid, double or redouble by a player required by law to pass, that call and subsequent legal calls stand; but if the offender was required to pass for the remainder of the auction, he must still pass at subsequent turns;

(c) a bid of more than seven, that call and all subsequent calls are cancelled; the offender must substitute a pass, and the auction proceeds as though there had been no irregularity;

(d) a call after the auction is closed, that call and all subsequent calls are cancelled without penalty.

36. Inadmissible Double or Redouble

Any double or redouble not permitted by Law 19 is cancelled and the offender must substitute a legal call; and (*penalty*) the offender's partner must pass whenever it is his turn to call (Law 23(c) may apply), and the lead penalties of Law 26(b) will apply if he becomes a defender.

If the right of the non-offending side to penalise is forfeited, Law 35 applies.

37. Bid, Double or Redouble in Violation of the Obligation to Pass

A bid, double or redouble by a player who is required by law to pass is cancelled, and (*penalty*) both members of the offending side must pass during the remainder of the auction (Law 23(c) may apply), and the lead penalties of Law 26 will apply if they become defenders.

38. Bid of More than Seven

No contract of more than seven is ever permissible. A bid of more than seven by any player is cancelled, and (*penalty*) both members of the offending side must pass during the remainder of the auction (Law 23(c) may apply); and the lead penalties of Law 26 will apply if they become defenders.

39. Call After the Auction is Closed

A call after the auction is cancelled, *and*:

(a) If it is a pass by a defender or any call by declarer or dummy, there is no penalty.

(b) If it is a bid, double or redouble by a defender, the lead penalties of Law 26 apply, unless the call has been condoned (*see* Law 35(d)).

40. Partnership Agreements

A player may make any call or play (including an intentionally misleading call such as a 'psychic bid', or a call or play that departs from commonly accepted or previously announced practice) without prior announcement, provided that it is not based on a partnership understanding. But a player may not make use of a bidding or play agreement unless;

(a) His side has disclosed its use of such call or play beforehand, *or*

(b) It has been agreed beforehand that the use of partnership understandings be disclosed at the time they are used. His partner must then disclose it. In this case, partner's disclosure must be confined to an indication that a partnership understanding has been used; he should not offer any explanation unless requested to do so.

Any group may restrict the use of special partnership understandings in its games.

PART VI

THE PLAY
CORRECT PROCEDURE

Law
41. Opening Lead, Review, Questions

After the auction closes,* declarer's LHO makes the opening lead. After the opening lead, dummy spreads his hand in front of him on the table, face up, sorted into suits, the cards in order of rank in columns pointing lengthwise towards declarer, with trumps, if any, to dummy's right. Declarer plays both his hand and that of dummy.

Declarer, before making any play, or either defender at his first turn to play, may require a restatement of the auction in its entirety.

After it is too late to have previous calls restated, declarer or either defender is entitled to be informed what the contract is and whether, but not by whom, it was doubled or redoubled.

Either defender may require an explanation of the partnership understanding relating to any call made by an opponent (*see* Proprieties 4), but only at that defender's own turn to play. Declarer may at any time require an explanation of the partnership understanding relating to any call or play made by a defender.

---

* After the final pass, either defender has the right to ask if it is his opening lead.

42. Dummy's Rights

Dummy is entitled to give information as to fact or law, but may not initiate the discussion; and provided he has not forfeited his rights (*see* Law 43) he may also:

(a) ask declarer (but not a defender), when he has failed to follow suit, whether he has a card of the suit led;

(b) try to prevent any irregularity* by declarer;

(c) draw attention to any irregularity, but only after play is concluded.

43. Dummy's Limitations

Dummy may not participate in the play (except to play the cards of dummy's hand as directed by declarer), or make any comment on the bidding, play, or score of the current deal; and if he does so, Law 16 may apply. During play, dummy may not call attention to an irregularity once it has occurred.

Dummy forfeits the rights provided in (a), (b) and (c) of Law 42 if he exchanges hands with declarer, leaves his seat to watch declarer play, or, on his own initiative, looks at the face of a card in either defender's hand; and if, thereafter:

(a) He is the first to draw attention to a defender's irregularity, declarer may not enforce any penalty for the offence.

(b) He warns declarer not to lead from the wrong hand (*penalty*) either defender may choose the hand from which declarer shall lead.

(c) He is the first to ask declarer if a play from declarer's hand constitutes a revoke, declarer must substitute a correct card if his play was a revoke, and (*penalty*) one trick is transferred to the defending side.

* He may, for example, warn declarer against leading from the wrong hand.

44. Sequence and Procedure of Play

The player who leads to a trick may play any card in his hand.* After the lead, each other player in turn plays a card, and the four cards so played constitute a trick.

In playing to a trick, each player must follow suit if possible. This obligation takes precedence over all other requirements of these Laws. If unable to follow suit, a player may play any card.*

A trick containing a trump is won by the player who has contributed to it the highest trump. A trick that does not contain a trump is won by the player who has contributed to it the highest card of the suit led. The player who has won the trick leads to the next trick.

45. Card Played

Each player except dummy should play a card by detaching it from his hand and placing it, face up, on the table where other players can easily reach and see it. Dummy, if instructed by declarer to do so, may play from his hand a card named or designated by declarer.[†]

A card must be played:

(a) If it is a defender's card held so that it is possible for his partner to see its face.

(b) If it is a card from declarer's hand that declarer holds face up, touching or nearly touching the table, or maintains in such a position as to indicate that it has been played.

(c) If it is a card in dummy deliberately touched by declarer except for the purpose of arranging dummy's cards

---

* Unless he is subject to restriction after an irregularity committed by his side.

[†] If dummy places in played position a card declarer did not name, the card must be withdrawn if attention is drawn to it before each side has played to the next trick, and a defender may withdraw (without penalty) a card played after the error but before attention was drawn to it (*see* Law 47).

or of reaching a card above or below the card or cards touched.

(d) If the player who holds the card names or otherwise designates it as the card he proposes to play. A player may, without penalty, change an inadvertent designation if he does so without pause for thought; but if an opponent has, in turn, played a card that was legal before the change of designation, that opponent may, without penalty, withdraw any card so played and substitute another.

(e) If it is a penalty card, subject to Law 50.

A card played may not be withdrawn except as provided in Law 47.

46. *Partial Designation of a Card to be Played from Dummy's Hand*

When a declarer instructs dummy to play a card from dummy's hand, as permitted by Law 45, but names only a suit or only the rank of a card, or the equivalent, without fully specifying the card to be played, declarer must complete his partial designation. Dummy must not play a card before declarer has completed his partial designation.

47. *Retraction of a Card Played*

A card once played may be withdrawn only:

(a) to comply with a penalty, or to correct an illegal play, or to correct the simultaneous play of two or more cards (*see* Law 58); if a defender's card which has been exposed is withdrawn under this sub-section, it becomes a penalty card (*see* Law 50); *or*

(b) after a change of designation as permitted by Law 45(d); *or*

(c) after an opponent's change of play, to substitute a card for one played;* *or*

---

* The offending side must not base any subsequent plays on information gained from such a withdrawn play.

(d) to correct a play* after misinformation by an opponent. A lead out of turn may be retracted without penalty if the leader was mistakenly informed by an opponent that it was his turn to lead.

PENALTY CARD

48. Exposure of Declarer's Cards

Declarer is not subject to penalty for exposing a card, and no card of declarer's or dummy's ever becomes a penalty card. Declarer is not required to play any card dropped accidentally.

When declarer faces his cards after an opening lead out of turn, Law 54 applies. When declarer faces his cards at any other time, he may be deemed to have made a claim or concession of tricks, in which case Law 68 applies.

49. Exposure of a Defender's Cards

Whenever a defender faces a card on the table, holds a card so that it is possible for his partner to see its face, or names a card as being in his hand, before he is entitled to do so in the normal course of play or application of the law, (penalty) each such card becomes a penalty card (see Law 50).†

50. Disposition of a Penalty Card

A card is a penalty card when prematurely exposed. It must be left face up on the table until it is played or until an alternate penalty has been selected.

---

* The offending side must not base any subsequent plays on information gained from such a withdrawn play.

† Exposure of a card or cards by a defender who is making a claim or concession of tricks is subject to Law 70.

A single card below the rank of an honour and exposed inadvertently (as in playing two cards to a trick, or in dropping a card accidentally) becomes a minor penalty card. Any penalty card of honour rank, or any card exposed through deliberate play (as in leading out of turn, or in revoking and then correcting) becomes a major penalty card; when one defender has two or more penalty cards, all such cards become major penalty cards.

When a defender has a minor penalty card, he may not play any other card of the same suit below the rank of an honour until he has first played the penalty card. (However, he is entitled to play an honour card instead of the minor penalty card.) There is no further penalty, but the offender's partner must not base any subsequent play on information gained through seeing the penalty card.

When a defender has a major penalty card, such card must be played at the first legal opportunity whether in leading, following suit, discarding or trumping. If a defender has two or more penalty cards that can legally be played, declarer may designate which is to be played. The obligation to follow suit, or to comply with a lead or play penalty, takes precedence over the obligation to play a penalty card, but the penalty card must still be left face up on the table and played at the next legal opportunity.

When a defender has the lead while his partner has a major penalty card, declarer may choose to impose a lead penalty at this point: he may require that defender to lead the suit of the penalty card, or may prohibit that defender from leading that suit (a prohibition continues for as long as he retains the lead). If declarer does impose a lead penalty, the penalty card is picked up at once. If declarer does not, the defender may lead any card; but the penalty card remains a penalty card. The defender may not lead until declarer has indicated his choice.

51. Two or More Penalty Cards

When a defender has two or more penalty cards in one suit, and declarer requires or prohibits the lead of that suit, the defender may pick up every penalty card in that suit and may make any legal play to the trick.

When a defender has penalty cards in more than one suit, declarer may prohibit the defender's partner from leading every such suit, or require him to lead one such suit; but the defender may then pick up every penalty card in every suit required or prohibited by declarer and may make any legal play to the trick.

52. Failure to Lead or Play a Penalty Card

When a defender is required by Law 50 to play a penalty card, but instead plays another card, he must leave the illegally played card face up on the table; *and*

(a) declarer may accept the defender's lead or play, and must do so if he has thereafter played from his or dummy's hand, but the unplayed penalty card remains a penalty card; *or,*

(b) declarer may require the defender to substitute the penalty card for the card illegally played, in which case the illegally played card becomes a major penalty card.

LEAD OUT OF TURN

53. Lead Out of Turn Accepted

Any lead out of turn may be treated by an opponent as a correct lead. It becomes a correct lead if an opponent accepts it by making a statement to that effect, or if that opponent next to play plays a card to the irregular lead.*

* When such a play is made by a defender who is not next to play after the irregular lead, Law 57 applies.

However, the player whose turn it was to lead – unless he is the offender's partner – may make his proper lead subsequent to the infraction without his card being treated as played to the irregular lead. The proper lead stands, and all cards played in error to this trick may be withdrawn without penalty.

54. Opening Lead Out of Turn
When a defender makes the opening lead out of turn:

(a) Declarer may accept the irregular lead as provided in Law 53. Dummy's hand is spread in accordance with Law 41, and the second card to the trick is played from declarer's hand; but if declarer first plays to the trick from dummy's hand, dummy's card may not be withdrawn except to correct a revoke.

(b) Declarer must accept the irregular lead if he could have seen any of dummy's cards (except cards exposed during the auction, subject to Law 23). He is deemed to have accepted the irregular lead if he begins to spread his hand as though he were dummy and in so doing exposes one or more cards; declarer must spread his entire hand, and dummy becomes declarer.*

(c) Declarer may accept the irregular lead by spreading his hand and becoming dummy; his partner becomes the declarer.

(d) Declarer may require the defender to retract his irregular lead (except as provided in (b) above), and then Law 56 applies.

55. Declarer's Lead Out of Turn
When declarer leads out of turn from his or dummy's hand;

(a) Either defender may accept that lead as provided in Law 53.

* If cards are so exposed from both declarer's and dummy's hands, the player who was regularly to become declarer remains declarer.

(b) Either defender may require declarer to retract that lead. *Then*,

   (i) if it was a defender's turn to lead, declarer restores the card led in error to his or dummy's hand, without penalty;

 (ii) if declarer has led from the wrong hand when it was his turn to lead from his or dummy's hand, he withdraws the card led in error; he must lead a card from the correct hand.

(iii) if declarer adopts a line of play that could have been based on information obtained through his infraction, the offenders should redress the damage in accordance with Proprieties 1.

56. *Defender's Lead Out of Turn*

When a defender leads out of turn:

(a) Declarer may accept that lead as provided in Law 53.

(b) Declarer may require the defender to retract that lead; the card illegally led becomes a major penalty card (*see* Law 50 – note that lead penalties are provided).

IRREGULAR LEADS AND PLAYS

57. *Premature Lead or Play by a Defender*

When a defender leads to the next trick before his partner has played to the current trick, or plays out of turn before his partner has played, (*penalty*) declarer may:

(a) require offender's partner to play his highest card of the suit led; *or*

(b) require offender's partner to play his lowest card of the suit led; *or*

(c) prohibit offender's partner from playing any card of one different suit specified by declarer.

Declarer must select one of these options, and if the offender's partner cannot comply with the penalty selected he may play any card, as provided in Law 59.

When, as a result of the application of the penalty, the offender's partner wins the current trick, he leads to the next trick; and any card led or played out of turn by the other defender becomes a major penalty card (Law 50).

A defender is not subject to penalty for playing before his partner if declarer has played from both hands; but a single-ton or one of two or more equal cards in dummy is not considered automatically played unless dummy has played the card.

58. Simultaneous Leads or Plays

A lead or play made simultaneously with another player's legal lead or play is deemed to be subsequent to it.

If a defender leads or plays two or more cards simul-taneously, and if only one such card is visible, he must play that card; if more than one card is exposed, he must desig-nate the card he proposes to play and each other card exposed becomes a penalty card (Law 50).

If declarer leads or plays two or more cards simul-taneously from either hand, he must designate the card he proposes to play and must restore any other card to the correct hand. If declarer withdraws a visible card and a defender has already played to that card, such defender may, without penalty, withdraw his card and substitute another (see footnote to Law 47).

If the error remains undiscovered until both sides have played to the next trick, Law 67 applies.

59. Inability to Lead or Play as Required

A player may play any otherwise legal card if he is unable to lead or play as required to comply with a penalty, whether because he holds no card of the required suit, or because he has only cards of a suit he is prohibited from leading, or because he is obliged to follow suit.

60. Play After an Illegal Play

A play by a member of the non-offending side after his RHO has played out of turn, and before a penalty has been imposed, forfeits the right to penalise the offence. The illegal play is treated as though it were in turn (but Law 53 applies to the player whose turn it was). If the offending side had a previous obligation to play a penalty card or to comply with a lead or play penalty, the obligation remains at future turns.

When a defender plays after declarer has been required to retract his lead out of turn from either hand, but before declarer has led from the correct hand, the defender's card becomes a penalty card (Law 50).

A play by a member of the offending side before a penalty has been imposed does not affect the rights of the opponents and may itself be subject to penalty.

THE REVOKE

61. Failure to Follow Suit – Inquiries Concerning a Revoke

Failure to follow suit in accordance with Law 44, or failure to lead or play, when able, a card or suit required by law or specified by an opponent in accordance with a penalty, constitutes a revoke. Any player may ask a player who has failed to follow suit whether he has a card of the suit led, and may demand that an opponent correct his revoke, except that dummy* may ask of declarer, but not of a defender (a claim of revoke does not warrant inspection of quitted tricks, except as permitted in Law 66).

* Unless he has forfeited his rights, as specified by Law 43.

62. Correction of a Revoke

A player must correct his revoke if he becomes aware of it before it becomes established (*see* Law 63). To correct a revoke, the offender withdraws the card he played in revoking and follows suit with any card. A card so withdrawn becomes a major penalty card (Law 50) if it was played from a defender's unfaced hand. The card may be replaced without penalty if it was played from declarer's or dummy's hand* or if it was a defender's faced card. Each member of the non-offending side may, without penalty, withdraw any card he may have played after the revoke but before attention was drawn to it (*see* footnote to Law 47). After a non-offender so withdraws a card, the hand of the offending side next in rotation may withdraw a played card, which becomes a major penalty card if played from a defender's hand.

On the twelfth trick, a revoke, even if established, must be corrected if discovered before the cards have been mixed together. If the revoke was committed by a defender before his partner has played to the twelfth trick, and if offender's partner holds cards of more than one suit, (*penalty*) declarer may then require the offender's partner to play to that trick either of the two cards he could legally have played.

63. Establishment of a Revoke

A revoke becomes established when the offender or his partner leads or plays (whether legally or illegally) to the following trick, or names or otherwise designates a card to be so played, or makes a claim or concession of tricks orally or by facing his hand. The revoke may then no longer be corrected (except for a revoke on the twelfth trick – *see* Law 62), and the trick on which the revoke occurred stands as played.

* Subject to Law 43. A claim of revoke does not warrant inspection of quitted tricks except as permitted in Law 67.

64. Procedure after Establishment of a Revoke

When a revoke has become established:

(a) If the offending player* won the trick on which the revoke occurred, (*penalty*) that trick and one of any subsequent tricks won by the offending side are transferred[†] to the non-offending side (if no subsequent trick was won by the offending side, only the revoke trick is transferred);

(b) If the offender's partner won the trick on which the revoke occurred, (*penalty*) that trick is transferred[†] to the non-offending side and, if the offending player himself won a subsequent trick with a card which could legally have been played to the revoke trick, one additional trick (but no more) is transferred[†] to the non-offending side.

(c) If the non-offending side won the trick on which the revoke occurred, and if the offending side won any trick after the revoke, (*penalty*)

   (i) The first such trick is transferred[†] to the non-offending side, and

  (ii) If the offending side won two or more tricks after the revoke, any of which was won by the offending player with a card he could legally have played to the revoke trick an additional trick is transferred[†] to the non-offending side;

(d) There is no trick penalty for the established revoke if,

   (i) The offending side did not win either the trick on which the revoke occurred or any subsequent trick; or if,

  (ii) The revoke was a subsequent revoke in the same suit by the same player; or if,

  (iii) The revoke was made in failing to play any card faced on the table, including a card from dummy's hand; or if,

  * If declarer revokes, but wins the trick on which the revoke occurred in dummy, Section (b) applies

  [†] For the scoring of transferred tricks, *see* Law 77.

(iv) Attention was first drawn to the revoke after all players had abandoned their hands and permitted the cards to be mixed together; or if,

(v) The revoke was on the twelfth trick (*see* Law 62).

N.B. When any established revoke, including one not subject to penalty, causes damage to the non-offending side insufficiently compensated by the law, the offending side should, under Proprieties 1, transfer additional tricks so as to restore equity.

TRICKS

65. Collection and Arrangement of Tricks

The cards constituting each completed trick are collected by a member of the side that won the trick and are then turned face down on the table. Each trick shall be identifiable as such, and all tricks taken by a side should be arranged in sequence in front of declarer or of one defender, as the case may be, in such manner that each side can determine the number of tricks it has won and the order in which they were taken.

66. Inspection of Tricks

Declarer or either defender may, until a member of his side has led or played to the following trick, inspect a trick and inquire what card each player has played to it. Thereafter, until play ceases, quitted tricks may be inspected only to account for a missing or surplus card. After play ceases, the tricks and unplayed cards may be inspected to settle an allegation of a revoke, of honours, or of the number of tricks won or lost. If, after an allegation has been made, a player on one side makes verification of the allegation impossible, as by mixing the cards or merging the tricks, the issue must be decided in favour of the other side.

67. Trick either Appropriated in Error or Defective.

A trick appropriated by the wrong side must, upon demand, be restored to the side that has in fact won it.*

A trick containing more or fewer than four cards is defective. When one player is found, during play, to have fewer or more cards than all the other players, the previous tricks should be forthwith examined, face down; if a defective trick is discovered, the player with a correspondingly incorrect number of cards is held responsible. The defective trick is inspected face up and

(a) Until the responsible player has played to a subsequent trick, the defective trick is rectified as follows:

(i) If the offender has failed to play a card to the defective trick, he adds to that trick a card he can legally play;

(ii) If the offender has played more than one card to the defective trick, he withdraws all but one card, leaving a card he can legally play;

(iii) The non-offending side may, without penalty, withdraw any cards played after the irregularity and before attention was drawn to it (*see* footnote to Law 47); but the offending side may not withdraw cards that constitute legal plays, and any cards they withdraw may become penalty cards (Law 50).

(b) After the responsible player has played to a subsequent trick, the ownership of the trick cannot be changed and

(i) If the offender has failed to play a card to the defective trick, he forthwith faces and adds a card to that trick, if possible one he could legally have played to it.

* If calls have been made on a subsequent deal, *see* Law 78.

(ii) If the offender has played more than one card to the defective trick, he withdraws all but one card, leaving the highest card he could legally have played to that trick. A withdrawn card may become a penalty card (Law 50); such a card is deemed to have belonged continuously to the offender's hand and failure to have played it to an earlier trick may constitute a revoke.

68. Declarer's Claim or Concession of Tricks

Declarer makes a claim or a concession whenever he announces that he will win or lose one or more of the remaining tricks, or suggests that play should be curtailed, or faces his hand. Declarer should not make a claim or a concession if there is any doubt as to the number of tricks to be won or lost.

69. Procedure Following Declarer's Claim or Concession

When declarer has made a claim or concession, play is temporarily suspended and declarer must place and leave his hand face up on the table and forthwith make a comprehensive statement as to his proposed plan of play, including the order in which he will play the remaining cards.

Declarer's claim or concession is allowed, and the deal is scored accordingly, if both defenders agree to it. The claim or concession must be allowed if either defender has permitted any of his remaining cards to be mixed with another player's cards; otherwise, if either defender disputes declarer's claim or concession, it is not allowed. Then, play continues.

When his claim or concession is not allowed, declarer must play on, leaving his hand face up on the table. At any time, either defender may face his hand for inspection by his partner, and declarer may not impose a penalty for any irregularity committed by a defender whose hand is so faced.

The objective of subsequent play is to achieve a result as equitable as possible to both sides, but any doubtful point must be resolved in favour of the defenders. Declarer may not make any play inconsistent with the statement he may have made at the time of his claim or concession. And if he failed to make an appropriate statement at that time, his choice of plays is restricted thereby:

(a) If declarer made no relevant statement, he may not finesse* in any suit unless an opponent failed to follow in that suit before the claim or concession, or would subsequently fail to follow in that suit on any conceivable sequence of plays.

(b) If declarer may have been unaware, at the time of his claim or concession, that a trump remained in a defender's hand, either defender may require him to draw, or not to draw, the outstanding trump.

(c) If declarer did not, in his statement, mention an unusual plan of play, he may adopt only a routine line of play.

If declarer attempts to make a play prohibited under this law, either defender may accept the play, or, provided neither defender has subsequently played, require declarer to withdraw the card so played and substitute another that conforms to his obligations.

70. Defender's Claim or Concession of Tricks

A defender makes a concession when he agrees to declarer's claim, or when he announces that he will lose one or more of the remaining tricks.

A defender makes a claim when he announces that he will

---

* For these purposes, a finesse is a play the success of which depends on finding one defender rather than the other with or without a particular card.

win one or more of the remaining tricks, or when he shows any or all of his cards for this purpose. If:

(a) The claim pertains only to an uncompleted trick currently in progress, play proceeds normally; cards exposed or otherwise revealed by the defender in making his claim do not become penalty cards, but Law 16, Unauthorised Information, may apply to claimer's partner.

(b) The claim pertains to subsequent tricks, play is temporarily suspended; the claimer must place and leave his hand face up on the table and make a comprehensive statement as to his proposed plan of defence. The claim is allowed, and the deal scored accordingly, if declarer agrees to it. If declarer disputes the claim, the defenders must play on with the claimer's hand face up on the table. Those cards do not become penalty cards. However, declarer may prohibit claimer's partner from making any play that could be suggested to him by seeing the faced cards.

71. Concession Withdrawn

A concession may be withdrawn:

(a) If a player concedes a trick his side has, in fact, won; or if declarer concedes defeat of a contract he has already fulfilled; or if a defender concedes fulfilment of a contract his side has already defeated (if the score has been entered, *see* Law 78).

(b) If a trick that has been conceded cannot be lost by any probable sequence of play of the remaining cards, and if attention is drawn to that fact before the cards have been mixed together.

(c) If a defender concedes one or more tricks and his partner immediately objects, but Law 16 may apply.

PART VII

THE SCORE

Law
72. Points Earned
The result of each deal played is recorded in points, which fall into two classes:

1. *Trick Points*. Only declarer's side can earn trick points, and only by winning at least the number of odd tricks specified in the contract. Only the value of odd tricks named in the contract may be scored as trick points (*see* Law 81). Trick points mark the progression of the rubber towards its completion.

2. *Premium Points*. Either side or both sides may earn premium points. Declarer's side earns premium points by winning one or more overtricks; by fulfilling a doubled or redoubled contract; by bidding and making a slam; by holding scorable honours in declarer's or dummy's hand; or by winning the final game of a rubber.* The defenders earn premium points by defeating the contract (under-trick penalty) or by holding scorable honours in either of their hands (*see* Law 81).

Each side's premium points are added to its trick points at the conclusion of the rubber.

73. Part Score – Game
The basic units of trick points are part score and game. A part score is recorded for declarer's side whenever declarer fulfils a contract for which the trick points are less than 100

---

* For incomplete rubber, *see* Law 80.

points. Game is won by that side which is the first to have scored 100 or more trick points either in a single deal or by addition of two or more part scores made separately. No part score made by either side in the course of one game is carried forward into the next game.

74. The Rubber

A rubber ends when a side has won two games. At the conclusion of the rubber, the winners of two games are credited with a premium score of 500 points if the other side has won one game, or with 700 points if the other side has not won a game. The trick and premium points scored by each side in the course of the rubber are then added. The side with the larger combined total wins the rubber, and the difference between the two totals represents the margin of victory computed in points.

75. Method of Scoring

The score of each deal must be recorded, and it is preferable that a member of each side should keep score.

Scores are entered in two adjacent columns separated by a vertical line. Each scorer enters points earned by his side in the left-hand column, and points earned by his opponents in the right-hand column.

Each side has a trick point score and premium score, separated by a horizontal line intersecting the vertical line. All trick points are entered, as they are earned, in descending order below the horizontal line (below the line), all premium points in ascending order above the line.

Whenever a game is won, another horizontal line is drawn under all trick point scores recorded for either side, in order to mark completion of the game. Subsequent trick points are entered below that line.

76. Responsibility for the Score
When the play of a deal is completed, all four players are equally responsible for ascertaining that the number of tricks won by each side is correctly determined and that all scores are promptly and correctly entered.

77. Transferred Tricks
A trick transferred through a revoke penalty is reckoned for all scoring purposes as though it had been won in play by the side to which it had been awarded.*

78. Correction of the Score
When it is acknowledged by a majority of the players that a scoring error was made in recording an agreed-upon result (e.g., failure to enter honours, or incorrect computation of score), the error must be corrected if discovered before the net score of the rubber has been agreed to. However, except with the consent of all four players, an erroneous agreement as to the number of tricks won by each side may not be corrected after all players have called on the next deal.

In case of disagreement between two scores kept, the recollection of the majority of the players as to the facts governs.

79. Deals Played with an Incorrect Pack
Scores recorded for deals played with an incorrect pack are not subject to change by reason of the discovery of the imperfection after the cards have been mixed together.

---

* Declarer plays in 3♡ and makes eight tricks. A revoke by a defender is found to have been established, with the offender having won both the trick in which the revoke occurred and a later trick. Two tricks are transferred from the defenders to declarer, who therefore has ten tricks. Since he bid only 3♡, he scores 90 trick points which count towards game, and 30 premium points from the overtrick.

80. *Incomplete Rubber*

When, for any reason, a rubber is not finished, the score is computed as follows:

If only one game has been completed, the winners of that game are credited with 300 points; if only one side has a part score or part scores in a game not completed, that side is credited with 100 points; the trick and premium points of each side are then added, and the side with the greater number of points wins the difference between the two totals.

81. *SCORING TABLE*

TRICK SCORE

Scored below the line by declarer's side, if contract is fulfilled:

	IF TRUMPS ARE			
For each trick over six, bid and made	♣	♢	♡	♠
Undoubled	20	20	30	30
Doubled	40	40	60	60
Redoubled	80	80	120	120

	AT A NOTRUMP CONTRACT		
	Undoubled	Doubled	Redoubled
For the first trick over six, bid and made	40	80	160
For each additional trick over six, bid and made..	30	60	120

The first side to score 100 points below the line, in one or more hands, wins a GAME. When a game is won, both sides start without trick points towards the next game. The first side to win two games wins the RUBBER POINTS.

PREMIUM SCORE
Scored above the line by declarer's side:

For winning the RUBBER, if opponents have won no
game 700
For winning the RUBBER, if opponents have won one
game 500
UNFINISHED RUBBER – for having won the only
            game 300
            for having the only PART
            SCORE in an unfinished
            game 100
For making any DOUBLED CONTRACT 50
or for making any REDOUBLED CONTRACT 100

SLAMS

For making a SLAM	NOT VULNERABLE	VULNERABLE
Small Slam (12 tricks) bid and made	500	750
Grand Slam (all 13 tricks) bid and made	1000	1500

OVERTRICKS

For each OVERTRICK (tricks made in excess of contract)	NOT VULNERABLE	VULNERABLE
Undoubled	Trick Value	Trick Value
Doubled	100	200
Redoubled	200	400

HONOURS

Scored above the line by either side:

For holding four of the five trump HONOURS
(A,K,Q,J,10) in one hand 100
For holding all five trump HONOURS in one hand 150
For holding all four ACES in one hand at a notrump
contract 150

UNDERTRICK PENALTIES

Tricks by which declarer fails to fulfil the contract; scored
above the line by declarer's opponents if the contract is not
fulfilled:

	Not Vulnerable		
	UNDOUBLED	DOUBLED	REDOUBLED
For first undertrick	50	100	200
For each additional undertrick	50	200	400
Bonus for the fourth and each subsequent undertrick	0	100	200
	Vulnerable		
	UNDOUBLED	DOUBLED	REDOUBLED
For first undertrick	100	200	400
For each additional undertrick	100	300	600

PART VIII

PROPRIETIES

1. GENERAL PRINCIPLES

The Laws cannot cover every situation that might arise, nor can they produce equity in every situation covered. Occasionally, the players themselves must redress damage. The guiding principle: the side that commits an irregularity bears an obligation not to gain directly from the infraction itself; however, the offending side is entitled to profit after an infraction, as an indirect result, through subsequent good fortune.*

---

* Two examples may clarify the distinction between direct gain through an infraction and indirect gain through good luck.

(a) South, declarer at 3NT, will have nine tricks available if the diamond suit – six cards headed by the ace, king, queen in dummy opposite declarer's singleton – divides favourably; and the six missing diamonds are in fact split evenly, three-three, between East and West. However, West, who holds three diamonds headed by the jack, shows out on the third round of diamonds, revoking. Thus, declarer wins only three diamond tricks instead of six, for a total of six tricks instead of nine. The established revoke is later discovered, so one penalty trick is transferred after play ends. But declarer is still down two.

Here, East-West gained two tricks as a direct consequence of their infraction. The players should adjudicate this result, scoring the deal as 3NT making three (Note, declarer is not given a penalty trick in addition; the object is to restore equity, to restore the result likely to have occurred had the infraction not been committed).

(b) South, declarer at 4♠, is entitled to require or forbid a diamond opening lead from West, because of an auction-period infraction committed by East. Declarer instructs West to lead a diamond – but West,

To infringe a law intentionally is a serious breach of ethics, even if there is a prescribed penalty that one is willing to pay. The offence may be the more serious when no penalty is prescribed.

There is no obligation to draw attention to an inadvertent infraction of law committed by one's own side. However, a player should not attempt to conceal such an infraction, as by committing a second revoke, concealing a card involved in a revoke or mixing the cards prematurely.

It is proper to warn partner against infringing a law of the game: for example against revoking, or against calling, leading or playing out of turn.

2. Communication Between Partners

Communication between partners during the auction and play should be effected only by means of the calls and plays themselves, not through the manner in which they are made, nor through extraneous remarks and gestures, nor through questions asked of the opponents and explanations given to them. Calls should be made in a uniform tone without special emphasis or inflection, and without undue hesitation or haste. Plays should be made without emphasis, gesture or mannerism and, so far as possible, at a uniform rate.

---

having no diamonds, leads another suit. East, now aware that partner is void in diamonds, is able to find what would be, under normal circumstances, a most unnatural line of defence to give West two ruffs. Thereby, East-West defeat a contract that would almost certainly have been made but for the infraction.

Here, East-West profited only indirectly through their auction-period infraction; their gain was the direct consequence of declarer's decision to require a diamond lead, and of West's lucky void. So, the players should allow the result to stand. Declarer was damaged, not by the infraction itself, but by bad luck afterwards – and luck is part of the game of bridge.

Inadvertently to vary the tempo or manner in which a call or play is made does not in itself constitute a violation of propriety, but inferences from such variation may properly be drawn only by an opponent, and at his own risk. It is improper to attempt to mislead an opponent by means of a remark or a gesture, through the haste or hesitancy of a call or play (such as hesitation with a singleton), or by the manner in which the call or play is made.

Any player may properly attempt to deceive an opponent through a call or play (so long as the deception is not protected by concealed partnership understanding). It is entirely proper to make all calls and plays in unvarying tempo and manner in order to avoid giving information to the opponents.

When a player has available to him improper information from his partner's remark, question, explanation, gesture, mannerism, special emphasis, inflection, haste or hesitation, he should carefully avoid taking any advantage that might accrue to his side.

3. Conduct and Etiquette

A player should maintain at all times a courteous attitude towards his partner and opponents. He should carefully avoid any remark or action that might cause annoyance or embarrassment to another player or might interfere with the enjoyment of the game. Every player should follow uniform and correct procedure in calling and playing, since any departure from correct standards may disrupt the orderly progress of the game.

As a matter of courtesy, a player should refrain from:

(i) Paying insufficient attention to the game (as when a player obviously takes no interest in his hand, or frequently requests a review of the auction).

(ii) Making gratuitous comments during the play as to the auction or the adequacy of the contract.

(iii) Detaching a card from his hand before it is his turn to play.

(iv) Arranging completed tricks in a disorderly manner, thereby making it difficult to determine the sequence of plays.

(v) Making a claim or concession of tricks if there is any doubt as to the outcome of the deal.

(vi) Prolonging play unnecessarily for the purpose of disconcerting the other players.

Furthermore, the following are considered breaches of propriety:

(a) Using different designations for the same call.

(b) Indicating approval or disapproval of a call or play.

(c) Indicating the expectation or intention of winning or losing a trick that has not been completed.

(d) Commenting or behaving during the auction or play so as to call attention to a significant occurrence, or to the state of the score, or to the number of tricks still required for success.

(e) Showing an obvious lack of further interest in the deal (as by folding one's cards).

(f) Looking intently at any other player during the auction or play, or at another player's hand as for the purpose of seeing his cards or of observing the place from which he draws a card (but it is not improper to act on information acquired by inadvertently seeing an opponent's card).

(g) Varying the normal tempo of bidding or play for the purpose of disconcerting another player.

(h) Mixing the cards before the result of a deal has been agreed upon.

4. Partnership Agreements

It is improper to convey information to partner by means of a call or play based on special partnership agreement, whether explicit or implicit, unless such information is fully and freely available to the opponents.

It is not improper for a player to violate an announced partnership agreement, so long as his partner is unaware of the violation (but habitual violations within a partnership may create implicit agreements, which must be disclosed). No player has the obligation to disclose to the opponents that he has violated an announced agreement; and if the opponents are subsequently damaged, as through drawing a false inference from such violation, they are not entitled to redress.

When explaining the significance of partner's call or play in reply to an opponent's inquiry, a player should disclose all special information conveyed to him through partnership agreement or partnership experience; but he need not disclose inferences drawn from his general bridge knowledge and experience. It is improper for a player whose partner has given a mistaken explanation to correct the error immediately or to indicate in any manner that a mistake has been made (he must not take advantage of the unauthorised information so obtained).

5. Spectators

A spectator, including a member of the table not playing, must not display any reaction to bidding or play while a hand is in progress (as by shifting his attention from one player's hand to another's). He must not in any way disturb a player. During the hand, he must refrain from mannerisms or remarks of any kind (including conversation with a player). He may not call attention to any irregularity or mistake, nor speak on any question of fact or law except by request of the players.

APPENDICES

1. Any group may specify that the Alert procedure be used in its games. Then, the partner of a player who makes a call to which the partnership attaches a special, unusual meaning, one with which the opponents may not be familiar, is required to say, "Alert." N.B., no explanation should be volunteered. After the Alert, either opponent may, at his own turn to call, inquire as to the special meaning.

   A partnership that does not want to be Alerted should so request; and this request should be honoured.

2. Any group may specify that the "Stop" or "Skip Bid" procedure be used in its games. Then, whenever a player opens the bidding at the two level or higher, or makes a bid higher than necessary to overcall the last preceding bid, he announces, "Stop," or "Skip Bid" (the group specifies the form to be used), before making the bid.

   After this announcement, the opponent next to speak is required to hesitate for approximately ten seconds before making any call.

3. Any group may specify that opening leads be made face-down in its games. If this opening lead is determined to be out of turn (before being faced), the leader returns the card to his hand without penalty.

   When the face-down lead will be legal, dummy delays spreading his hand. Opening leader's partner asks any questions concerning the auction, including a review. Then, the lead is faced (opening leader may not withdraw it), dummy is faced, and play proceeds normally.